ADVENT BEGINS
AT HOME

Family Prayers and Activities
for Advent and Christmas

Compiled by
David Polek, C.SS.R.
and
Rita Anderhub

Liguori
ONE LIGUORI DRIVE
LIGUORI MO 63057-9999

Imprimi Potest:
Edmund T. Langton, C.SS.R.
Provincial, St. Louis Province
The Redemptorists

Imprimatur:
John N. Wurm, S.T.D., Ph.D.
Vicar General, Archdiocese of St. Louis

ISBN 0-89243-111-3

Cover design and Illustrations: Jim Corbett

Our thanks go to all who contributed prayers, activities, and ideas for this
booklet and especially to Sister Janet Crane, O.SS.R., and the people of Mary,
Mother of the Church parish, St. Louis, Mo.

To order, call 1-800-325-9521
www.liguori.org or catholicbooksonline.com

TABLE OF CONTENTS

Introduction

That *time* of the year is here again — when the air gets crisper, the days grow shorter, and just about everyone's thoughts turn to Christmas.

In the past, the Christmas "season" started officially with Thanksgiving. But today the Christmas decorations appear right after Halloween, sometimes sooner. And every year we hear the cry raised far and wide, "We must get the spirit back into Christmas! What can we do to really prepare?"

Advent is the season when we should take time to think about the *why* of Christmas — why all the decorations, why all the preparation, why all the hustle and bustle, the buying and selling? It should be a time to look within our hearts to see if there is anything that stands in the way of Jesus' coming.

If Advent is to mean anything for us today, the meaning must come from family and home. Attending Sunday Mass together is one way of preparing; the Advent liturgies are beautiful with their imagery and their gentle air of anticipation for the one "who is to come."

This booklet was prepared to help people — parents, children, teachers, students — live the spirit of Advent. Our hope is that these suggested ways of preparing and celebrating will help all to realize whose coming we are celebrating on December 25.

ADVENT IS A TIME TO WAIT

All precious things take time to grow. This is true of love within a family; it is also true of anything that grows.

The trouble with growing and waiting is that so much depends on how much we want what we wait for, and what we want badly we want right now. A coach wants a fine football team immediately. A lonely person wants to hear a friend knock at the door right now. A politician is eager to know the outcome of an election, even before the voting begins. The more we want the pot of gold at the end of the rainbow the longer the rainbow seems.

Advent is often here and gone and we scarcely know it has happened. Something is wrong. Advent, which means "coming," puts the world back into the time of darkness before Christ. It is waiting for the Light which is Christ, waiting for life. From the darkness of hundreds of years of promise there is a faint voice of someone in the wilderness calling, "I come." In the four weeks of Advent the cry becomes louder and louder and our waiting should be more and more filled with expectation and hope. This should be somewhat like the feelings and hopes of parents about to have their first child. They can hardly wait in their expectation of such a wonderful event.

ADVENT IS A TIME TO HOPE

For a long time now people have been linking faith, hope, and love together. This is how it should be. Take for example a forester who reseeds great stretches of burned-out land after a forest fire. He plants the seeds hoping they will grow, expecting them to grow. He has faith that they will grow. He believes the rain and the ashes of the fire will be the food of new life for the young seeds. But he would have none of these attitudes if he did not love the trees and the forests in the first place.

The prophets of the Old Testament acted in the same way. They not only hoped the Savior would come, they fully expected it. They believed he would come. It is a rather simple matter to say, "I hope it happens," while not really expecting that it will. But those who really believe are willing to work for, and to wait for what they fully expect to happen.

And so the world waits for Christ. It expects him. It believes he will come. Christ will plant a seed, much like the forester. He will sow the seed of his work, which is to bloom into the Church and spread to the four corners of the earth with its life-giving fruit, with its saving message.

ADVENT IS A TIME TO GROW

Have you ever noticed a young person prepare for an important date? What would a girl or a boy do without a mirror? Carefully, she applies every bit of makeup; she checks the way her dress looks; she brushes every strand of hair neatly into place. He checks out all his various looks, flashing them into the mirror to see if he is duly impressive. What does not pass inspection is quickly changed.

People look into mirrors in anticipation of an important event, whether it is a date, a party, or a service. The season of Advent is much like that. There is a great event breaking on the dawn. We are all invited. Many will ignore the knocking at their doors, but it is for them. Those who would prepare themselves need a mirror as well, the interior mirror of the heart.

Advent is a time to enrich the heart. It is a time for interior growth as we eagerly look forward to the coming of Christ. It bids us pause to consider the inner beauty which is the kingdom of God.

The hostess of a dinner party scrupulously inspects the table to see that every knife and fork is in place, every crystal glass is sparkling, every napkin spotlessly clean. Would that our hearts would undergo such an inspection. Would that we were as concerned with greed, injustice, selfishness, as men and women are with wrinkles, stains, and smudged glassware.

We lament that the commercial world has taken over and the Christ again can find no home. But there is something we can do about that. We can cease to ignore the spiritual or religious aspects of Advent and Christmas. The sharpness of the air makes our bodies move more quickly—inviting us to action. And the knowledge that we are awaiting Emanuel, the one "who is to come," sharpens our spiritual consciousness as we strive to truly celebrate Advent and Christmas.

PART ONE: PRAYERS

1. Advent Prayer Wreath

A custom which children love and which daily and visibly expresses the meaning of the Advent season is the Advent wreath. The light of the candles reminds us that Christ is the Light of the world. The circular shape reminds us that God is eternal, that is, he had no beginning and will live forever. The evergreens remind us that God never changes.

The Advent wreath can be made and used in a number of ways. An ordinary Christmas wreath may be placed on a table with four candles in low holders. Evergreen boughs may be fastened to an Advent wreath frame. Frames are available at religious goods stores or they can be made as part of a family project. Greens may also be wired to a circle shaped from an old coat hanger.

Three of the candles for the wreath are purple, the fourth one, lighted on the third Sunday of Advent, is rose or pink to express our joy that Christmas is so close. If all four candles are white, three purple bows and one pink bow may be tied around the candles.

There is no definite way to use the Advent wreath. Each family (or class) will discover the procedure that works best for them. On the eve of the first Sunday of Advent, or the Sunday itself, the family gathers around the wreath, the prayers are said (see below for Advent prayers), and each child in turn lights the first candle. Some families have the wreath on their dining table and light the candles before they say their meal prayers. Others place it on the TV or on an end table in the living room and say their night prayers as a family around the wreath. A class might put the wreath on the windowsill of the classroom or on a small table so everyone can see it.

Each week one more candle is lit. The gathering light in the wreath each week announces that the celebration of Christ's coming draws steadily near.

2. Advent Prayers for Each Day

(The following could be an instruction about the meaning of the Advent wreath and could be read as is to the family, or the head of the household could give it to the family in his/her own words.)

Soon our family will be getting ready for Christmas. Just like Dad and Mom are getting our house decorated and you children are doing things in school to get ready for Christmas, we all must get ready in another way. Each one of us has a body and a soul; and since Jesus lives in us, we must get ourselves ready for Christmas. We do this during the time of something called Advent, which means "coming." Who do you think is coming soon? The answer, of course, is Jesus.

We have four weeks to go before Jesus will be born; so we have four candles on our wreath, one for each week and one big white one in the middle. Each week we will light one candle and by Christmas we will have them all lit. Then on Christmas day we will light just the one white candle and sing "Happy Birthday" to Jesus, just like we sing to each other on our own birthdays.

Let's look at our wreath now and see how it is made and why it is made that way. We used these green branches called evergreen, which means they always stay green. The color green on Mass vestments symbolizes life; and the *ever* green on the wreath reminds us that God's love for us never changes and our love for God never changes.

The wreath is in a circle because a circle has no beginning and no end. If you drew a circle around a penny on a piece of paper and then took the penny away, you probably wouldn't know where you started or where you ended. This circle means our life with God just keeps going; he keeps loving us and we should always love him.

We already said there are four candles because there are four weeks before Jesus will be born. Three of the candles are violet. The color violet represents sorrow. During Advent we will say that we are sorry for not loving Jesus enough and that we will try hard to do better. The pink or rose candle means joy or happiness that Jesus will be coming to us again at Christmas. When we light the candles, this stands for Jesus being the Light of the world. His teachings are our guiding light. If we listen to what he wants us to do, we will be happy with him forever. The one white candle in the middle of the circle stands for the Christ Child, born on Christmas day.

We will use our wreath every day to help bring us closer to God and to make us more loving children of God.

FIRST WEEK OF ADVENT: EXPECTATION

(These paragraphs at the beginning of each week can be read aloud or used as the material for a little explanation.)

This first week of Advent has to do with a big word called "expectation." When you look carefully at the word, there is a smaller word in there — can you find it? It is "expect." When you expect something to happen, you wait for it to happen. We are waiting for Christ to come to us at Christmas. Could we have Christmas without Christ? Of course not. It is only because of Christ that we have Christmas at all. Since we know the exact time of his coming, we know how much time we have to prepare for him. When we have company we don't do everything at the last minute. Maybe we clean one part of the house one day and another part the next day. Then we might cook some of the food one day or do the baking on another day. We should work the same way in preparing our hearts and souls for Jesus by working on different things each day until he arrives. That way we'll be all ready for him when he comes.

(The Advent wreath ceremony is simple. It starts at the evening meal on the Saturday before the first Sunday of Advent with the blessing of the wreath. The head of the household is ordinarily the one to say the prayers; and the various members of the family take turns lighting the candles. Each night before supper, the following prayers could be used or ones made up by members of the family.)

BLESSING. O God, please bless our wreath and be with us as we prepare our hearts for the coming of Christ. As we light the candles each day, help us remember to keep our hearts lit with your love. Amen.

SUNDAY:

We hear the glad sounds around us of people preparing for the coming of Jesus. We thank you, Jesus, for coming each year in a special way. During this month, everyone seems more loving and kind. Through prayers, help us to keep this feeling of joy all year long. God the Father has sent you to us to know, to love, and to serve you. If sometimes we forget, please help us.

MONDAY:

Thank you, God, for this beautiful world you have given us — the day and the night, the sky with its sun, moon, and stars, the earth with its trees and plants, the waters with its fish. Thank you for the animals of every kind, and for all the people you put here for us to love. When we feel sad or sick, please watch over us, and help us to remember to call upon you. We know that there are good days and bad days, happy times and sad times, sick feelings and well feelings, and that you are with us through all these times if we ask you to be. Please stay with us.

TUESDAY:

Dear God, help us to say we are sorry when we are wrong. Help us to say "that's OK" when someone hurts us. Help us to say "I still like you" when someone is mean to us. Help us to say "I love you" when we know someone does not love us. All of this will be hard to do, but we will try.

WEDNESDAY:

Dear God, you send your bright dawn to light up the lives of all men and women. Please, God, help us to be strong to do what you ask. Help us to make Christ welcome when he comes this Christmas.

THURSDAY:

Help us to be kind to others and to treat them as we would want them to treat us. Keep us from the feelings inside us at times to do wrong and to hurt others. Help us to not speak badly about others.

Give us faith, which is believing in God and what he teaches, and peace to fight against fear. Hold us in your hand and help us to know that you are with us.

FRIDAY:

What can we give you, God? You have everything already. What do you want most of all from us? We give you what we think is most important — ourselves — our hearts, our minds, and our souls. Take them, Lord.

SATURDAY:

O Lord, as we reach the end of our first week of Christmas preparation, we thank you for letting us know you a little better.

We learned that the word Advent means coming and stands for the coming of Jesus.

We learned that Advent starts four weeks before Christmas and lasts until Christmas Eve. That is why there are four candles. We learned that the candles stand for Christ, the Light of the world. He is our guiding light.

We learned the wreath is covered with evergreen, because this particular tree always stays green. It never changes, just like God's love for us and our love for God never change. Green is the color of life and growth, and we pray to God to bring us closer to him and to help us stay alive and grow in faith and love.

We learned that the violet color of the candles stands for the sorrow we have for the wrongs we have done. We know God loves us and will forgive us if we are truly sorry. We learned that God has come to deliver us from all evil and will give us a place with him in heaven if we live like he wants us to.

We thanked him for this beautiful world he has given us — the trees, flowers, snow, and sunshine. We asked him to help us use these things in a nice way and not to hurt others with them.

We asked him to help us forgive others when they hurt us.

We asked him to help us love others when they do not love us.

We asked him to help us be kind to others and treat them as we would want them to treat us.

We asked him to protect us.

And after this whole week, we offer him our hearts, which are now cleaner and holier than they were a week ago.

SECOND WEEK OF ADVENT: HOPE

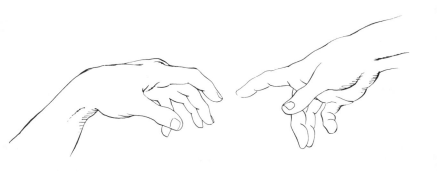

The second week of Advent has to do with hope. We are still waiting for and preparing for Jesus' coming and hoping to make Jesus a part of our lives, not just at Christmas but all year long. We can prepare ourselves for Jesus through prayer and turning ourselves to love, hope, faith, justice (treating people right), and kindness. Prayer opens our hearts to let God, love, and faith in, and lets out our hate and fear. Prayer is like a window through which the light of God shines through. Let us this week continue in hope and prayer to keep this window open.

SUNDAY:

O God, thank you for this day you have made. Help us to be kinder to one another in our home and friendlier to the people around us. Help us to do right and avoid doing wrong.

MONDAY:

O God, thank you for our mother and father, our sisters and brothers. Thank you for our friends. We will try harder this week to help one another be happy.

TUESDAY:

O God, help me when I feel angry and mean and sad. Help me when I feel like I hate someone or something.

WEDNESDAY:

Lord, help me to live my day like you would want me to. Help me to help my mom and dad, like you helped your mom and dad, Mary and Joseph. Help me to be like you, loving and caring.

THURSDAY:

Help me, God, to know my religion. Help me to understand how I can know, love, and serve you. You are always with me, and you know when I am scared and in trouble. Please bring me closer to you at these times through my religion and through those who love and care for me.

FRIDAY:

Dear Jesus, we know we get a special strength from you when we confess our sins and receive Communion and when we pray. We need this strength, called grace, to make our souls grow stronger and to stay healthy, just like our bodies need food to keep them growing and healthy. Teach us to use this grace when we feel like being bad or doing something wrong — by asking you for your help right away. Remind us to call upon you in time of temptation.

SATURDAY:

This week has been filled with hope, our hope that the spirit of Christmas will fill our hearts all year. Knowing that you, Lord, are always ready to forgive us, even though we don't deserve it, we look forward to celebrating Jesus' birthday.

THIRD WEEK OF ADVENT: JOY

This third week of Advent we light the pink or rose candle which means joy. From Jesus Christ we have received so much love, beauty, and joy for the simple things in life. This week let us be happy with simple things that don't cost money — like reading a book instead of watching television, like talking to one another instead of playing games, listening to the children laugh instead of talking on the telephone, eating plain food instead of having fancy desserts. Remember that the purple candles stand for sorrow that we have done wrong. But now we are joyful, because the time for the arrival of Jesus is almost here.

SUNDAY:

Our Father, thank you for letting us celebrate Jesus' birthday again. Help us to be like him, so when people look at us they see goodness and beauty like we see in Jesus.

MONDAY:

Dear Jesus, help us to know you better, love you more, and follow your rules. When we look at the lights of the Christmas tree, help us to think that you are the true Light of the world. Help us to remember that you are with us to guide us and cheer us.

TUESDAY:

O God, at times it is hard to remember you, especially around this time when we think of the house decorations, Christmas cards, and gifts we're going to receive. And sometimes, even though we have all these beautiful things around us and all the people around us, we still feel alone and scared. Help us to remember that it is because of you we have this Christmas celebration and that you are always with us and we can trust in you to take care of us. Help us truly believe that you will forgive our sins, give us new life, and look after us after we die.

WEDNESDAY:

O God, before you sent Jesus to us we were lost and alone. You showed us how much you loved us by sending Jesus to die on the Cross for our sins, and you asked us to share your love with others. During this time help us to spread your name to others by telling them about you and by showing them how you want them to live. Make us examples of your love.

THURSDAY:

Thank you, Lord, for the joy we feel because you are with us. May we share this joy with the people we meet at work, at school, at church, at the store, and everywhere.

FRIDAY:

We thank you for the gifts you give us at Christmas, the gifts you can't put in a box with a ribbon on it. We thank you for the gift of Christ, bringing us new life. For the gift of our home. For the gift of our dad, who works hard for us. For the gift of our mom, who does so many things for us. For the gift of our children, who make us so happy with their smiles and questions. For the gift of our friends, who are so good to us. For the gift of our grandmas and grandpas, who do so much for us. For the gift of school and religion, that we may learn more and more every day.

SATURDAY:

In this week of Advent we learned there are many joys to have without spending any money. We learned to look around and enjoy the things and people around us. We learned we don't always need to be doing something or going some place to have fun. We learned there are many things we can give people and get from people, things that don't come in boxes with bows on them.

FOURTH WEEK OF ADVENT: ACCEPTANCE

This fourth week of Advent has to do with acceptance, which means saying "yes" to someone who asks us to do something. When God asked Mary to be the mother of God, she said "yes." She didn't say, "Just a minute" or "Let me think about it" or "I'll tell you if I want to or not after this TV program is over." No, she just said "yes."

This week is our chance to say "yes" to God through our families and friends, even though a "no" would be much easier at times. When we want to say "no," we should try to remember that God might like us to say "yes." And every time we do say "yes" we will be closer to God because acceptance is pleasing to him.

SUNDAY:

Today we thank you, Lord, for giving us people who can tell us about you and your coming. We thank you for our priests and teachers and everyone who talks about you in a loving way. Help us to pay attention so we may live the way you have shown us.

MONDAY:

Dear God, Christmas is almost here. Once more we give you the gift of our hearts. We wrap ourselves in grace and love and tie our gift with a big effort to do good always. Help us, Lord, to give you one whole week of not yelling, crying, arguing, fighting, or being mean. We will really try to be nice to one another all this week, and then on Christmas morning each of us can say, "I did this for you, Jesus, and now I give myself to you."

TUESDAY:

O God, who sent us your only Son, Jesus, help make this Christmas the most beautiful one we have ever had. Teach us to think first of giving ourselves to you before we think of getting presents. Remind us that Jesus will come to us this Christmas and make us better persons, and fill us with love that we can share with people all year long.

WEDNESDAY:

O God, we stand here in front of you knowing we cannot keep secrets from you. You know all about us, and you know how we feel. When we feel like being ugly toward someone, may your beauty help us not to. When we feel like hating someone, may your love help us not to. When we feel like being mean, may your goodness help us not to. You are our light; please show us the way.

THURSDAY:

Great God, you have come to us and you give us Jesus. Even when it is hard to listen to how we should act, help us to follow you and find love and grace. Teach us to pray and listen to you.

FRIDAY:

God the Father, we thank you for Jesus. By believing in and loving him, Christmas comes every day. Help us to remember this Christmas all year long by giving the presents of life: love, patience, kindness, and understanding.

SATURDAY:

Lord, in this fourth and last week of our Christmas preparation, we have thanked you for the people who believe in you and who can tell us about you.

We have given ourselves to you and will try to go on giving of ourselves, because we know it is better to give than to receive.

We accept your love for us and know it will last forever. Your love is so much better than any present we could receive, because it will not break or wear out but will go on and on.

We have come a long way from the very first night of Advent. At that time we lit the very first candle. The next week there were two, then three, and finally four candles shining very brightly, just like our love for you is shining very brightly. We pray our love for you goes on shining forever. And now we are back to one candle. As we light it we say, "Happy birthday, Jesus."

3. Family Prayer Center

Advent has always been a time to think more about the life of Jesus and our own life and how we can become more like him. Because of this, we seem to pray more often, by ourselves and with our family. To help families to pray, it is suggested that you choose a special place in your home where you can go to pray individually or as a family.

Choose an unused corner somewhere in your home where there is a shelf or where you can put a small table. After covering the table, place a Bible and candles on it. Other aids to prayer may be added—a crucifix, a statue of a favorite saint, a plant.

After the prayer center is set up, gather together as a family during Advent to dedicate and bless this as a place for each person and the family to come closer to the Father.

4. Advent Prayer Services

Selfishness, greed, and pettiness are found to some degree in every family. These offenses tend to destroy the unity of the family. They can stifle its growth. If the members recognize their need to root out these tendencies and to grow in love, then they certainly must recognize the need for prayer.

Advent is a special time for quiet, deep reflection in private, as well as prayer in common with the other members of the family.

The following prayer services could be used any time — before meals, as night prayers, etc. These three services are to be used as starters. Perhaps you and your older children or class will continue along the same vein and plan other prayer services you could use.

PRAYER SERVICE ONE

(Place an unlit candle on a table. Gather the family around. Darken the room.)

(The head of the household explains that the darkness reminds us of what it was like before Jesus came to live here on earth. When Jesus came to earth he was good and kind to others. He showed people how to love one another. He made this world a happier place; that is why we call Jesus the Light of the world. [Light the candle.] Jesus is still with us, but we cannot see him. Jesus will come into our hearts in a special way on Christmas day. Let us pray so that we will be ready for him.)

Leader: That we may be more thoughtful of others.
All: Come, Lord Jesus.
Leader: That we may help others to know you better.
All: Come, Lord Jesus.
Leader: That we may learn to be unselfish.
All: Come, Lord Jesus.
Leader: That all people may know you as Savior.
All: Come, Lord Jesus.
Leader: O God, our Father, we are waiting for your Son to come to us. Help us to see him when he comes to us in the words of our priests, in the love of our families, and in the daily events of our work and play.
All: Amen.

PRAYER SERVICE TWO

(Start with a Bible reading: Luke 1:26-38, from a Children's Bible if possible, or read the following.)

In the sixth month the angel Gabriel was sent by God to a town in Galilee called Nazareth, to a virgin betrothed to a man named Joseph, of the House of David; and the virgin's name was Mary. He went in and said to her, "Rejoice, so highly favored. The Lord is with you." She was deeply disturbed by these words and asked herself what this greeting could mean, but the angel said to her, "Mary, do not be afraid; you have won God's favor. Listen. You are to conceive and bear a son, and you must name him Jesus. He will be great and will be called Son of the Most High. The Lord God will give him the throne of his ancestor David; he will rule over the House of Jacob for ever and his reign will have no end." Mary said to the angel, "But how can this come about, since I am a virgin?" "The Holy Spirit will come upon you," the angel answered, "and the power of the Most High will cover you with its shadow. And so the child will be holy and will be called the Son of God. Know this too: your kinswoman Elizabeth has, in her old age, herself conceived a son, and she whom people called barren is now in her sixth month, for nothing is impossible to God." "I am the handmaid of the Lord," said Mary. "Let what you have said be done to me." And the angel left her.

(A few minutes could be allowed just to think about what has been read or to talk about the reading. Then the following prayers may be said.)

Leader: Mary received you into her heart.
All: Come into our hearts, Lord Jesus.
Leader: That we may love your Father as Mary does.
All: Come into our hearts, Lord Jesus.
Leader: So that we may be more like you.
All: Come into our hearts, Lord Jesus.
Leader: So that we may recognize you in everyone.
All: Come into our hearts, Lord Jesus.
Leader: So that we may love others more.
All: Come into our hearts, Lord Jesus.
Leader: O Mary, you were the first to receive Jesus into your heart. Pray to God for us that we may be as ready as you were to listen to God's word and to receive his Son into our hearts.
All: Amen.

PRAYER SERVICE THREE: A LIGHT SERVICE

(Gather the family around you. Place a tall candle in the center of the group. Light the candle and darken the room and the whole house.)

"What would it be like to be all alone in the dark?"

"If you were lost in a woods at night, what kind of light could you use?"

"Why would even a little light make you feel better?"

"Remember how all the people waited for the Promised One to come? They needed him and he was not yet with them. Sometimes they felt as we do if we are alone in the dark. Jesus wanted to be the light of the world. He said, 'I have come to be the light of the world.

23

Anyone who follows me will not walk in the dark.' "

"Christmas is the feast of Jesus. He came to be our light. Let us follow the light with our eyes, our feet, our hands, and our whole hearts." (The leader should walk in front of the family holding the candle up high. Upon returning to the living room, he should call each child by name and have him/her light a small candle from the large one. As each lights his/her candle, the leader says:)

"Jesus said, 'I am the light of the world; anyone who follows me will not walk in darkness.' "

(The whole family answers:) "Jesus, Light of the world, we welcome you."

(The whole family should then gather around the tall candle and listen while the father reads the Gospel of the birth of Christ from the Bible or from a Children's Bible.)

In those days Caesar Augustus published a decree ordering a census of the whole world. This first census took place while Quirinius was governor of Syria. Everyone went to register, each to his own town. And so Joseph went from the town of Nazareth in Galilee to Judea, to David's town of Bethlehem — because he was of the house and lineage of David — to register with Mary, his espoused wife, who was with child.

While they were there the days of her confinement were completed. She gave birth to her first-born son and wrapped him in a manger, because there was no room for them in the place where travelers lodged.

There were shepherds in that locality, living in the fields and keeping night watch by turns over their flocks. The angel of the Lord appeared to them as the glory of the Lord shone around them, and they were very much afraid. The angel said to them: "You have nothing to fear! I come to proclaim good news to you — tidings of great joy to be shared by the whole people. This day in David's city a savior has been born to you, the Messiah and Lord. Let this be a sign to you: in a manger you will find an infant wrapped in swaddling clothes." Suddenly, there was with the angel a multitude of the heavenly host, praising God and saying,

"Glory to God in high heaven,
peace on earth to those on whom his favor rests."

When the angels had returned to heaven, the shepherds said to one another: "Let us go over to Bethlehem and see this event which the Lord has made known to us." They went in haste and found Mary and Joseph, and the baby lying in the manger; once they saw, they understood what had been told them concerning this child. All who heard of it were astonished at the report given them by the shepherds.

Mary treasured all these things and reflected on them in her heart. The shepherds returned, glorifying and praising God for all they had heard and seen, in accord with what had been told them.

When the eighth day arrived for his circumcision, the name Jesus was given the child, the name the angel had given him before he was conceived" (Luke 2:1-21).

(All blow out their candles.)

5. Special Feast Days in Advent

There are many special days in Advent. Here are three that could be especially remembered as part of your Christmas preparation.

ST. NICHOLAS DAY (DECEMBER 6)

On the eve of St. Nicholas' Day parents might first read or tell to their children the story of kind St. Nicholas — how he provided dowries for poor girls, how he is the patron saint of Russia and the special protector of children. Then they might explain the custom of children (especially if they have been good) hanging stockings on the bedroom door or putting shoes outside the bedroom to receive gifts from St. Nicholas.

When the children put their shoes at the door or hang up their stockings, a list of what they want for Christmas might be tucked inside. In this way, the preoccupation with gift-getting is removed somewhat from the preparation for Christmas. Parents (or St. Nicholas!) can fill the shoes or stockings with a single item for each child that would be used in the family's preparation for Christmas. For example, a record of Christmas music of a spiritual nature, a Christmas calendar, a box of Christmas cards, a crib set, a

Christmas book, etc. A bit of candy or a few cookies might also be included, because St. Nicholas knew what people would like. This is a preview of Christmas. It is good because, while reminding the children of a saint, this custom intensifies their anticipation of Christmas.

IMMACULATE CONCEPTION (DECEMBER 8)

Here parents might explain the meaning of this day and what is celebrated — that it was Mary who (as a special favor from God) was conceived without stain of sin in preparation for the birth of his Son.

That day the family should go to Mass and then in the evening pray together around a lighted candle that has been decorated to honor the Mother of Jesus. A plain white or blue ribbon will make the candle special. Perhaps part of the rosary or some other favorite prayer to the Blessed Mother could be prayed.

ST. JANE FRANCES DE CHANTAL (DECEMBER 12)

Another interesting saint who would fascinate any child is Jane Frances de Chantal. She was wife, mother, nun, and the founder of a religious community. Frances died more than 300 years ago, but, while living, was a woman of beauty and refinement, lively and cheerful in temperament. Her life was not an easy one. Three of her six children died in infancy; her husband was killed; and she had to deal with a very fierce father-in-law.

Perhaps you might talk about St. Jane Frances with your children. What would Christmas have been like 300 years ago with her family? No electric lights. No gaudy presents. No television programs. No Santa Claus on city street corners. It could be a fine opportunity, not only to find out about a truly exemplary female saint but also to get a little perspective again on what and who we are celebrating.

6. Personal Checkup

Here are some questions for private reflection concerning yourselves and the people with whom you live. They can be used at any time, but particularly just before Christmas or as a little meditation on how you can improve yourselves in the coming year.

Perhaps you could spend some time in your place of prayer thinking of one or many of these questions or in the car on the way to work, etc. The important point is to make time during the last week of Advent or just before January 1 to examine your conscience and to pray and reflect on the following points.

• What's my best time of day?
• What's my worst time of day?
• Would I like to live with me at my worst time of day?
• What's my tone of voice when I talk to my family, my friends, people I want to impress?
• Am I generous in sharing my possessions with my husband, wife, brothers, sisters, sons, daughters, relatives, friends, neighbors?
• Am I equally generous of my time with my husband, wife, brothers, sisters, sons, daughters, relatives, friends, neighbors?
• After work, am I eager to get home? Why? Why not?
• How do I welcome family members when they come home? Would they know I'm glad to see them?
• When was the last time I hugged a member of my family for no particular reason except love?
• How do I feel when I think about hugging my husband, wife, son, daughter, sister, brother, mother, father?
• How do I feel when someone in my family sincerely compliments me?
• How do I feel about our family praying together?
• When was the last time someone in the family helped me out without being asked? How did that make me feel?
• When was the last time I helped someone in the family without being asked? How did that make me feel?
• What specifically could I do to improve our family time together?

7. A Family Celebration of Reconciliation

The following might be used as a little prayer service before New Year's Eve — to examine what might have gone wrong in the past year and to look at the new year to see how all in the family might do better. This can be led by the head of the household.

Reading: Psalm 32:1-7

Prayer: Let us pray.

Loving Father, you sent Jesus your only Son to die on the Cross and to restore life through his Resurrection. Help us to see your love in his sacrifice. As we express our sorrow for sin, may we return to you in loving service. We ask this through your Son who lives and loves with you and the Spirit forever.

All: Amen.

Petitions:

For the times we argue with each other.

Response: Lord have mercy.

For the times we fail to listen to each other. ℟

For the times we fail to reach out to each other in love. ℟

For the times we take each other for granted. ℟

For the times we put each other down. ℟

For the times we fail to do our best work. ℟

Reading: Psalm 28:6-9

Blessed be the Lord, for he has heard the sound of my pleading; the Lord is my strength and my shield. In him my heart trusts, and I find help; then my heart exults, and with my song I give him thanks. The Lord is the strength of his people, the saving refuge of his anointed. Save your people, and bless your inheritance; feed them, and carry them forever!

Prayer: Let us pray.

Leader:

Merciful Lord, we thank you for the gift of your never-ending love. Through your sacrifice you have freed us from sin. Father, Son, and Spirit, all glory and honor is yours today and forever.

All: Amen.

8. A New Year's Family Penance Service

The week after Christmas provides a great opportunity to get ready for the new year. This means reflecting upon the past year and setting some goals and limits and resolutions for the new year. The following is a family penance service designed to help families think over the past year, be honest with one another, and set goals for the future.

Someone begins the ceremony with this prayer:

Father and our Lord, Jesus Christ, be present among us now as we come to ask forgiveness for the wrongs we have done to each other during the past year and as we make our promises to change in the coming year. Help us to be honest. Help us to be kind to each other. Help us to be forgiving, and help us to know how to start over. Amen.

Next each family member speaks and says:

I ask your forgiveness for some of the following things that may have hurt you during the year . . . .

The next section begins with each family member asking:

I ask each of you to tell me, please, how you can help me during the coming year.

Then a prayer is offered by all:

Father, forgive us for the many times we have hurt each other. Help us to know the meaning of forgiveness. We know so well each other's faults, but we know just as well how to forgive and how to be forgiven. We promise before you and before each other to grow in holiness and in love within our family. Give us the courage and the strength to continue on in that love which we know to be supportive and understanding. Amen.

PART TWO: ACTIVITIES
1. Straw for the Crib

This custom, which seems to have originated in France, helps children see their efforts as they prepare for the coming of Jesus with many acts of kindness.

First, an empty crib is given a place of honor somewhere in the home, preferably a place people must pass often each day.

Each child in the family (and parents also) may place a piece of straw or yellow yarn in the crib each night for every kind act he/she did during the day.

The figure of the Christ Child is not placed in the crib until Christmas Eve. By that time the crib should be filled with soft straw or yellow yarn as a bed for the Child.

2. Advent Daily-Use Calendar

Here is a calendar to use daily during the season of Advent. Each day there is a suggestion for an activity, a family discussion, or a Bible reading to share and discuss. Some of the activities can be done individually, and all of them can be done together. The centerfold of this booklet is an example of this kind of calendar. This can be removed and put in a prominent place — on the bulletin board, taped to the refrigerator, or on the kitchen door. Everyone takes turns reading the suggestion for the family that day. Or do *your* family thing, an activity or discussion that is meant just for your family. You could even sit down together and figure out practices for each day for your own family to do. Here are some ideas on what to write.

1	— Write a Christmas letter to someone.
2	— Do not be afraid — I am with you! I am your God — let nothing terrify you! (Is 41:10)
3	— Draw a picture of someone waiting for something special.
4	— Make a Christmas poster this week.
5	— Sing a new song to the Lord. Sing to the Lord, all the world (Ps 96:1).
6	— Tell or write a story about preparing for Christmas. Share your story with someone else.
7	— Think quietly for five minutes about the people you love.
8	— The trees in the woods will shout for joy when the Lord comes to rule the earth (Ps 96:12-13).
9	— Give away one of your best smiles.
10	— Call or write your grandma or grandpa today.
11	— Think quietly for five minutes about the gifts you have received in your life.
12	— Sing heavens. Shout for joy earth. The Lord will comfort his people (Is 49:13).

13	— Write down or draw three things you hope for. Talk them over with a friend.
14	— Say "I'm sorry" to someone you've hurt.
15	— Do something for your mom or dad without being asked.
16	— Start a family discussion with: What does Advent mean to me?
17	— Offer to help an older neighbor with an odd job.
18	— Pray today for all who are lonely.
19	— Make straight in the wasteland a highway for our God! (Is 40:3)
20	— Take time to compliment your parish priest on his homily.
21	— Draw a picture of Bethlehem and the place where Jesus was born.
22	— Forgive someone who has hurt you.
23	— Begin a family discussion by asking: Why is Christmas worth waiting for?
24	— Ask at a family discussion: Why do you think waiting is meant to be a part of life?

25 *Christmas!*

3. Advent Calendar

Advent calendars may be bought at most religious bookstores. One "window" is opened each day of the Advent season. On Christmas day the whole Nativity scene is visible through the various "windows."

Advent calendars can also be made at home. Cut the appropriate number of perforated "doors" or "windows" (one for each day of Advent) on a piece of construction paper. Paste the construction paper over a picture of the Nativity. Each day of the Advent season a door may be folded open and gradually the whole scene unfolds.

You may also use an ordinary daily calendar. The dates are marked off for Advent in large, blank boxes. Every day each child and, perhaps, each parent may write one thing he/she did that day to get ready for the coming of Jesus.

4. Family Bulletin Board

Older children love to make a family bulletin board, updating it according to season. Construction paper cutouts, magazine pictures and captions, snapshots, or pictures drawn by younger children could be used to remind the entire family of the seasonal theme. Pictures could illustrate such themes as "Advent is a time of waiting," "From darkness to light," "Come, Lord Jesus," etc.

Another adaptation of the family bulletin board is a Christmas collage. A large piece of construction paper may be used for pictures or other objects to remind the family of Christmas. Photographs of loved ones may be pasted on it, or slips of paper with the good deeds of the family members written on them may be attached to it. At the end of Advent the board would be a graphic reminder of the good deeds done by family members for each other during Advent.

5. Bible Story Prayers and Activities

(During Advent we await the coming of Jesus. We learn about Jesus from the Bible. Many stories there tell us about him, and the following two can help prepare us for Christmas. The questions for discussion and the related activities also help us in our preparation.)

ZECHARIAH AND ELIZABETH (LUKE 1:5-24; 39-80)

THE STORY:

A long time before Jesus was born, God told his people that Jesus would come. Some people believed God and did not forget what he said. They told their children and their grandchildren about God's promise. They waited and waited for Jesus to come.

Two people, especially, were waiting for Jesus to come. Zechariah and Elizabeth, in their old age, sometimes felt lonely while they were waiting because they did not have any children of their own.

For years they had prayed to God that they could have children, but now they felt it was too late.

One day, though, something very wonderful happened. Zechariah went to the temple to pray. As he was praying, an angel came to him. "I have good news for you. God has heard your prayer. You and Elizabeth are going to have a baby boy. God wants you to call him John. When he grows up, he will tell people about Jesus, the Savior who is coming soon."

Zechariah could not believe his ears. "How can what you say be true?" he asked. "Elizabeth and I are too old to have a son."

Because Zechariah doubted God's message, the angel said, "I will give you a sign to show you that what I have told is true. You will not be able to speak until the baby is born."

Sure enough! Zechariah hurried home to tell Elizabeth what had happened, but when he got there, he couldn't talk. Now he believed that what the angel had told him really would happen.

However, Zechariah had to wait almost a whole year before he could talk again. Shortly after the baby was born, friends came to visit. They kept asking what the baby would be called. Some of the friends suggested names, but Zechariah took a tablet of slate and wrote, "His name is John."

Suddenly Zechariah's voice returned and he was able to speak. He was so happy that he burst out in praise of God.

QUESTIONS FOR DISCUSSION:
1. What had Zechariah and Elizabeth always hoped for? (A child of their own.)
2. Why didn't Zechariah believe what the angel told him? (He doubted the angel's word because he thought he and Elizabeth were too old to have a child.)
3. What was to be special about the child? (He was to grow up to tell people about Jesus.)
4. Why do you think the angel told Zechariah that he wouldn't be able to speak until the baby was born? (Because Zechariah doubted, the angel wanted to give him a sign that what he had told Zechariah would really happen.)
5. If you were Zechariah, what would be the first thing you would say when your voice came back again?

RETELLING THE STORY:

Your children absorb more of the feelings and attitudes of the story as they retell it in their own words. As you listen, you can evaluate what they have learned.

RELATED ACTIVITIES:

1. Terrycloth Board:
   To make the retelling of the story more vivid and more fun:
   — Suggest that your children draw the figures of Zechariah, Elizabeth, the angel, and a couple of neighbors.
   — Have them cut these figures out and glue a strip of coarse sandpaper on the back of each.
   — Place a terrycloth bath towel over an upright object, such as a blackboard, easel, or even a stiff piece of cardboard. The figures will adhere to the terrycloth.
   — Have the children take turns retelling the story as they move the figures about on the towel.
2. Pantomime:
   As you or one of your older children retell the story, let other members of the family pantomime the facial expressions, moods, and actions described by the narrator of the story.

MARY AND THE ANGEL (LUKE 1:26-38)

THE STORY:

Besides Zechariah and Elizabeth, there was another person who was waiting for the Promised One to come and who also received some "good news" from an angel. Her name was Mary, and she lived in the tiny town of Nazareth.

One day the angel Gabriel came to Mary and said, "Hail, Mary," which means, "Hello, Mary."

Mary looked up full of wonder at what she saw before her.

"Don't be afraid, Mary," Gabriel said. "You are the chosen one of God. God wants you to be the mother of his Son, the Savior for whom everyone is waiting. You should name the baby Jesus. Will you do what God asks?"

"Yes," said Mary. "I will do whatever God wants." Mary's heart was bursting with joy. She wanted to tell someone the good news.

Mary thought about Zechariah and her cousin, Elizabeth. She would go to visit them and tell them the wonderful news.

Elizabeth saw Mary coming over the hills and called out, "How lucky I am that the mother of the Savior should come to visit me!"

Mary hugged Elizabeth. "Rejoice with me," she said, "for God has done wonderful things for me."

QUESTIONS FOR DISCUSSION:

1. In what ways are the story of Zechariah and Elizabeth and the story of Mary alike?
2. In what ways are the stories different? (Zechariah doubted; Mary believed.)
3. Why did Mary go to visit Zechariah and Elizabeth?

RETELLING THE STORY:

Suggest that your children draw the story characters and cut them out of construction paper. Paste the cutouts on Popsicle sticks and use them as puppets in the retelling of the story.

RELATED ACTIVITIES:

1. Cut figures of Mary and the angel out of colored construction paper. Paste them on another piece of construction paper. Hang the picture somewhere in the house so that everyone may see it.
2. Draw a picture of Mary visiting Elizabeth.
3. Read to your children the story of Mary's Annunciation and Visitation from St. Luke's Gospel.

6. Advent and Christmas Banner or Poster

As a family or class, plan together a banner or poster on an Advent theme. Words such as "Come, Lord Jesus," "Rejoice," or "Advent 19 __ __" could express the theme of the banner or poster.

A banner or poster may be made simply by cutting the figures and letters out of felt and gluing them onto either felt or burlap or a big piece of poster paper or board. If felt is used for the banner, you can make an Advent banner on one side and a Christmas banner on the other. The Christmas banner could express the theme "Jesus is here." Hang the banner or poster somewhere in the house or the classroom where all can see it. It makes no difference whether the result is pretentious or plain. What is significant is that the family or class prepares, as a community, for the coming of the Lord.

7. Secret Friends and What to Do for Them

Advent is a time when you can seek for opportunities to give yourselves to others. Part of this giving can be done in secret by having a secret friend and by giving to that person. At the beginning of Advent, each family member writes his or her name on a piece of paper, and the names of all are put in a bowl. Each person draws a name out, and this person becomes his/her secret friend until Christmas. (Of course, if you draw your own name, you put it back and try for another.) It is important to keep the name a secret.

You look for ways to give of yourselves to your secret friend: by helping with his/her work, by writing little notes, by giving small gifts, and by praying especially for that person. All of these things are to be done secretly, but somehow they often become known.

Be on guard against performing religious acts for people to see. Otherwise expect no recompense from your heavenly Father. When you give alms, for example, do not blow a horn before you in synagogues and streets like hypocrites looking for applause. You can be sure of this much, they are already repaid. In giving alms you are not to let your left hand know what your right hand is doing. Keep your deeds of mercy secret, and your Father who sees in secret will repay you (Mt 6:1-4).

As that great day of Christmas draws near, work at making a special card for your secret friend. It can be made of construction paper and decorated as lavishly as possible. A loving message is included, and this time sign your name.

On Christmas Eve or the next day, put your card at your secret friend's place, and you will finally learn who has been doing all those nice things for you all during Advent.

Here are some things you can do for your secret friend:
— Offer to help with a job your friend has to do.
— Offer to do jobs for him/her.
— Write a note telling him or her about the qualities or talents he/she has that you like. (Don't sign the note!)
— Compliment your secret friend.
— Take time to listen to your friend.

— Pray for his or her intentions.
— Give your friend a small, secret gift.
— Give thanks to God for him/her.
— If necessary, say "I'm sorry."
— If your friend is lonely, ask if you can help.
— Give your secret friend the gift of your smile.

8. Giving Yourselves to the Poor

One of the special joys each of us has experienced is the pleasure we feel when we have done something nice for somebody else. We experience our own goodness when we are able to give the little extra that helps another person. Somehow, knowing we are good helps us to give even more and be even better.

Early in Advent, a family or a class might put two or three rolls of pennies in an open jar, placed where it is available to the group but not to passersby. Next to this jar, place a closed box with a slit in the top. This box can be decorated in any manner you choose. Whenever anybody in the family or class does something nice for someone else, he/she goes quietly and secretly to the open jar and transfers a penny into the box. On Christmas, the box of pennies is taken to church as a donation for the poor. It becomes an offering of yourselves and also of your resources.

41

9. Giving Yourselves to Others

(These suggestions can be written down, cut out, folded, and put in a container near the jar of pennies and the box.)

— When family members come home from work or school, greet them with a big hug.
— Make cleaning (the basement, garage, shed, barn) a family project.
— Mom and Dad, spend some time alone with each of your children.
— Put Dad's tools back where they belong.
— Have a family night, with the children planning the menu and activity.
— Mom and Dad, offer to help children with their work — cleaning rooms, dishes, setting table, whatever.
— Let Dad read the newspaper first; or leave it — in good order — where he can find it.
— Help another person with his/her work.
— Do your work before you are reminded.
— Offer to help with the laundry.
— Offer to help in the kitchen.
— Smile at your sisters and brothers.
— Let someone else have the biggest piece of dessert.
— Help someone with his/her schoolwork.
— Play a game with a younger brother or sister.
— Read to a younger brother or sister.
— Go to bed without fussing or playing around.
— Call or write to grandparents to say "I love you."
— Let others watch a TV program they want, even if it isn't your choice.
— Visit someone who is lonely or sick.
— Write a letter to a friend who has been waiting to hear from you.
— Compliment your dad, mom, sister, brother, or classmate on some special quality they have.
— Remember the magic words: "please," "thank you," "you're welcome," "I'm sorry."
— Thank your dad, mom, sister, brother, teacher, or classmate for the little things they are doing for you.

10. Planting a Narcissus Bulb

Since Advent is a season of waiting, children will really feel and live the spirit of this season if they are able to experience for themselves what it means to wait and to hope for something.

For this experience you will need a bag of pebbles and a paper-white narcissus bulb for each child. Both of these things can be bought at any florist or garden store.

A. Explain to your children or class that it will take about four weeks for the bulbs to bloom (the length of the Advent season).

B. Let the children place their bulbs together in a bowl of pebbles and water. The bulbs should be covered about halfway with water. This water level should be maintained throughout the four weeks.

C. Place the bowl in a dark closet, under the bed, or, better yet, in a cool, dark place in the basement for three weeks. Throughout the three weeks, as the children watch for signs of growth:

— Encourage them to express how much they wish they could see the green stem shooting up out of the pebbles;

— Explain to them that the roots are developing now in the darkness and that this period of waiting in darkness is necessary if the plant is ever to bloom;

— Compare the darkness and the growth of the roots to the years before Christ was born, when God was preparing his people for the birth of the Savior.

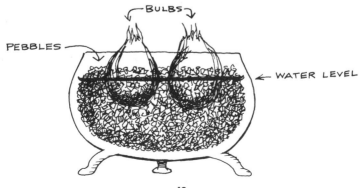

D. At the beginning of the fourth week you may remove the bowl from the dark place. However, it should not be placed in the sunlight for a few days. It can be placed in the sunlight when the tops turn a bright green.

Hopefully, you will have narcissus blooms in your home or classroom for Christmas day!

11. Christ Mobile

There are many ways to prepare the house for Christmas. One is to make a mobile as an Advent or Christmas decoration. The mobile illustrated here indicates how this can be done. Quotations from the Bible can be written — in color — on paper or light cardboard. Then tie them with string to a coat hanger and hang the mobile in some appropriate spot. It can be put up any time in Advent and is especially nice for all of the Christmas season.

It might be nice for the whole family or class to look up these Bible references and even substitute others for the ones given here.

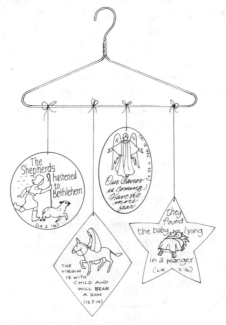

12. Candy Ribbon

Waiting is never easy, and waiting for Christmas seems to be extremely difficult, especially for little children. This project (and the next one) is for the little ones. The ribbons described here are to be placed on the bedroom doors of the children, as a sign of the passing of time.

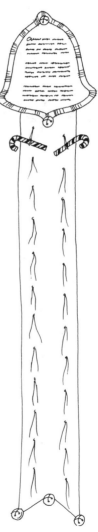

The candy ribbon is easy to make. Cut the form of a bell out of felt or paper. Hang a few tiny (real) bells on the felt, so the children can hear them ring when the door opens or closes. Place this near the top of the door. Then hang a three feet long by four inches wide piece of green or red felt from the felt bell. On this strip of felt tie 24 candy canes. Each day, from December 1 through December 24 the child will take one candy cane from the felt. When the canes are all gone it is time for Christmas.

Over the top of the bell you could put the following poem:

December 1st 'til Christmas
Is the longest time of year!
Seems as though old Santa
Just never will appear.

How many days 'til Christmas?
It's mighty hard to count.
So this little candy ribbon
Will tell the exact amount.

Untie a candy every night
When the sandman casts a spell
And Santa will be here
By the time you reach the bell.

13. Paper "Waiting" Ribbon

This is a simple variation of the candy ribbon. The idea is similar; it is meant to be a special sign that the days before Christmas are passing. The background can be felt, burlap, paper, etc. At the top, using one of last year's Christmas cards, the children can paste scenes of the Nativity. Then each child cuts out loops from construction paper and pastes them together to form a chain of 24 links — one for each day from December 1 through December 24.

This can be attached to a bedroom door, to the door leading to the family room, or wherever it can be seen and used each day. Each day one of the loops is clipped off and when there are no more loops it is Christmas! For variation, quotations from the Bible or some recommended act of kindness may be written on the loops.

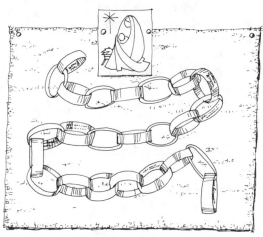

14. Collage

To celebrate the ways you have shared in Christ's coming on earth you can make a collage as a Christmas decoration for your home or the classroom. First, think about one thing you yourself have done during Advent that makes you especially proud; then think about one thing you as a family have done that makes you feel especially proud. Write these two things down on separate pieces of paper. Everybody in the family or class should prepare two slips of paper.

The edges of your paper can be torn, pinked, cut at different angles, or shredded to create different effects. Your accomplishments can be written in colors, and decorations can be added. Make them as fancy as you like, because they are special gifts from you.

When all have finished, paste the slips of paper onto a 9 x 12 (or larger) piece of construction paper. The slips of paper can be arranged at random, in the shape of a cross or a candle, whatever pleases you.

Display your collage in a prominent place in your home during the Christmas season. This is a beautiful reminder of your individual and family efforts during Advent to be more loving, grow closer to each other, and share the life of your family with others.

15. Christmas Crossword Puzzle

Crossword puzzles are one of today's most popular games. Children, as well as adults, enjoy working them. Here is "A Crossword Christmas."

Across

1. What you hang up by the chimney.
2. Silent _____.
4. The reindeer pull this.
6. You can build this with the snow.
8. What Santa wears on his feet.
9. It shook like a bowl full of jelly.
11. You hang these on your Christmas tree.
13. What you find under your Christmas tree.
17. We wish you a

_____ _____ .

21. Rudolph had a very shiny one.
22. Something we put up and decorate in our house.
23. What Santa carries on his back.
25. Rhymes with boys and we ask for them at Christmas.
26. _____ the snowman.
29. What presents are tied with.
30. Where you sit when you tell Santa what you want for Christmas.
31. The little guy who helps Santa make things.

32. Santa comes down this to bring our gifts.

Down

1. This person is making a list and checking it twice.
3. How Santa Claus laughs.
5. Some people put these on the outside of their house at Christmas.
7. Sometimes mothers let you help bake these.
10. A bowl full of _____ .
12. It's fluffy and white and is on Santa's face.
14. Santa Claus had eight of these.
15. Jingle _____ .
16. Sometimes it is on the very top of the Christmas tree and it rhymes with far.
18. The mailman brings these around Christmas.
19. It's sweet and good to eat.
20. We wish you a happy _____ _____ .
24. Red and white candy.
26. The place where you burn logs.
27. It's white and falls from the sky.
28. Where Santa Claus lives.

16. Journey to Bethlehem

The journey of Mary and Joseph to Bethlehem can be reenacted during the last week of Advent. The Mary and Joseph figures from the family crib set are taken to the top room or to the room farthest away from where the crib is placed. Forming a procession, the family sings carols as they carry the figures each day closer to the empty crib.

On Christmas Eve, the family gathers for the final procession to the crib. The youngest child leads the procession and carries the Mary and Joseph figures, followed by parents and other children carrying lighted candles and singing (*O Come, O Come Emanuel*, for example). The Mary and Joseph figures are then placed in the crib. Before going to bed that night the parents place the Christ figure in the crib, to be joyously discovered in the morning. The mood of the morning is indeed *Joy to the World!*

17. A Road to Bethlehem

Another way to impress upon children's minds the story of Mary and Joseph traveling such a long way is to make a road to the holy city of Bethlehem.

Using a large piece of paper or cardboard to be taped on a door or tacked to a bulletin board, you can draw a road of stepping stones leading to a picture of the Nativity. (A picture from last year's Christmas cards will serve the purpose.) The road may be used in two ways. Twenty-four stones can be drawn, so that each day a stone can be colored to mark the time until Christmas. Or many stones can be drawn so that a child may color one each time he does something that will bring him closer to Jesus. This could include positive and wholesome activities like telling Mom and Dad how much they are loved, remembering to say "thanks," reading from the Bible, doing a kind deed for a brother or sister, etc.

18. Homemade Ornaments and Decorations

Tree-trimming is an important part of the preparation for Christmas. The evergreen has always symbolized long life; in fact, it was originally a pagan custom which was canonized by Christianity. Everyone recognizes that the charm and beauty of a Christmas tree warms even the coldest and most unresponsive of hearts.

For this reason the tree should be a family project. In decorating your tree don't be afraid to take all evening, or a couple of evenings. Use your imaginations in making special ornaments. As children grow up, perhaps every year they could make a set of ornaments. Or a child could make one special ornament each year and save it to be used yearly as a reminder of how the family is growing up.

Garlands can be made by stringing popcorn or cranberries or making paper loop chains. Each personal ornament or decoration is a reminder that you are a family and are doing your best to look forward to and to enjoy this holiday celebration.

19. The Christmas Play

During Advent preparations can be made for the family's annual Christmas play. This is rather an ambitious project, but children love to give little plays. This event could be a joint project of all the cousins to be presented at the grandparents' house, perhaps on Christmas Eve.

An aunt or uncle can select the play and appoint the parts and arrange for simple props and costumes. Plays and stories are available from the library.

It is important to include the Nativity scene as part of the play. The baby might possibly be a live baby Jesus. Most children will take their parts very seriously. Older children can sing or help the younger ones with their parts. Invitations can be extended to the relatives, and a special one could be given to the grandparents. Admittedly, this is a difficult project, but it could become a popular and heartwarming family tradition.

20. Tree Decorating and Blessing

In order to bless a tree, you should remember that a tree can also bless you. For that to happen you need to come to know the tree. Let all the members of the family gather around the tree, before it is decorated, and take a good look at it. If it is a cut tree, look at its trunk and try to tell how old it is — one ring stands for one year. Count the branches; look closely at the needles; feel them, let them tickle you. Smell the pine scent. You could give the tree some water as one in the family reads this prayer.

> O Father and Creator of this most special tree which has come to our family, help us to be ever-mindful to feed and give drink to each other as we now feed and give drink to this tree. Help us to know that we receive life from each other, that we need each

other, and that we need most especially to remember each other at this season. Amen.

Next, while the tree is being placed in its stand, the following prayer may be said by the head of the household.

Father and Provider of our home, as we give this tree a home within our house, help us to remember the homeless and the poor at Christmastime. Help us to be ever thankful that we are together as a family and that we shelter each other. Finally, help us to make our house a happy home. Amen.

When it is time to decorate your tree and as the first string of lights is placed, one family member may read this prayer:

Jesus, Lord of light, we stand in awe as we take our own parts in bringing light to this tree. We know the meaning of you as the Light of the world, but we can never fully understand just how far that light can reach and into how many corners it needs to be brought. Help us this Christmas season not to hide our own lights under bushel baskets, but to shine them before all — to be radiant, happy, and loving people — showing forth your light in our very faces. Amen.

21. Special Gifts for Christmas

Many years ago most gifts were handmade, and the delicacy of the work made the gift much more appreciated. Today, as prices go up, more and more people are making gifts, baking cookies, etc. to express their good wishes at Christmas. Here are two easy things for children to make.

DECORATED CANDLES

You will need plain white candles, carving tools, felt-tipped pens, poster paints, brushes, colored paper, ribbons.

Decorate the candle by drawing and painting on it with the felt-tipped pens or poster paints. If you want a carved design on your candle, draw it first with pencil. (The designs shown here may help you.) Gently scratch the design into the wax, gradually cutting as deep as you want to go. Make sure you leave the candle resting on a smooth surface as you work so it won't break.

Now use the felt-tipped pens or the poster paints to color the design on your candle. Fold and cut colored paper to make a candle holder or tie a ribbon around the candle.

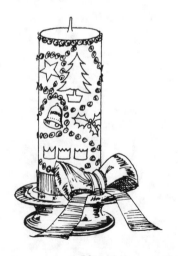

CANDLESTICKS

You will need some clay, some seeds — dried peas, lentils, pumpkins seeds, or fairly big sharp seeds from the garden. You can buy seeds at health-food or whole-food shops.

Knead the clay until it is smooth. Shape it into a cone or a flattened ball. Make a depression in the top to hold a candle. Now start making a design on the candlestick by pressing in the seeds. If you choose sharp pointy seeds and press the sharp end into the clay, they will stick better.

Spray or paint the candlestick with lacquer as soon as you have finished. Leave the bottom and the depression for the candle unlacquered so the clay can dry.

22. Christmas Baking

It is always a thrill for a child to see something he/she has made, whether it be a Christmas card, a banner, or something to eat. Christmas baking is an old tradition that has revived in recent years. Children love to bake. Let them make a mess. Let them enjoy themselves. You'll be surprised at the results. It might even be a good idea to let Dad take part and help with the baking. Here are some unusual examples of Christmas baked goods.

LEBKUCHEN (LIFE CAKE)

1⅓ cups honey	¼ tsp. each: nutmeg, cloves
¼ cup water	1¼ tsp. cinnamon
2 cups brown sugar	1½ cups shredded orange peel
4 eggs	1 cup candied lemon peel, chopped fine
6 cups flour	½ cup candied cherries, chopped fine
½ tsp. soda	2 cups chopped blanched almonds
⅛ tsp. salt	

Boil sugar, honey, and water for five minutes. Beat in eggs. Add sifted dry ingredients, stir in fruit and nuts. Cover, and let stand overnight. Roll ¼ inch thick. Cut into rectangles or squares large enough to cut a Christmas scene on. For instance: Cut shapes of St. Joseph, Mary, the shepherds, crib with Jesus, wise men, etc. Bake at 350° for about 10 minutes. Put a sugar glaze on them or a lemon-flavored confectioners icing.

BUTTERHORNS

1 lb. butter (real butter)	⅓ cup milk
1 lb. flour (about 4 cups)	1 tsp. sugar
2 egg yolks	(filling)

Cut up butter, flour, and sugar with a blender or knife. Make a well in it, add egg yolks and milk, and mix. Shape into a ball of dough and chill. Roll very thin, small portions at a time. Cut into 2 inch squares, fill with 1 tsp. filling (mixture of ground walnuts and sugar; ratio is ¾ cup sugar to 2 cups ground nuts) fold over, shape into crescents. Bake at 350° for 10 min. Sprinkle with confectioners sugar.

NUTS

SUGAR

WATER

GLAZED NUTS

Toast 3 cups of shelled almonds or walnuts in a heavy iron skillet in the oven, stirring occasionally. Melt 2 cups sugar and ½ cup water over low heat in heavy skillet or kettle. Do not boil. Stir in nuts, coat thoroughly. Spread out on wax paper to dry and crystalize sugar.

MORAVIAN HEARTS

This cookie can be a gift for the Feast of the Immaculate Conception, as well as for Christmas.

¼ cup melted butter	1⅞ cups flour
½ cup warm molasses	⅓ tsp. each: soda, salt, ginger,
½ cup brown sugar	cloves, cinnamon
⅛ tsp. each:	
nutmeg, allspice	

Mix butter, molasses, and sugar. Add sifted dry ingredients and roll thin. Cut with large heart-shaped cutter. Bake at 375° for 6 minutes. Ice with almond-flavored or other confectioners frosting.

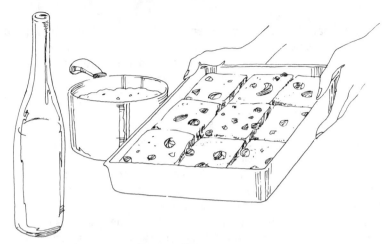

CANNOLI (ITALIAN FRUIT CAKE)

Cut a loaf of sponge cake into thin slices. Butter a square pan. Dip each piece in sherry or white wine. Some cooks use both, on alternating pieces. Line bottom of pan with slices. Spread them with quince, apricot, or apple jam on which drop a little candied fruit. Top this with another layer of cake. Cover all with a thick custard filling. Sprinkle with ground nuts and top with whipped cream. Serve in squares, topped with a colorful decoration: cherry, nut, greenery, or birthday candle. (A confession: Bakery sponge cake, and instant vanilla pudding for custard, we find, speed up preparation of this elegant and rich dessert!)

23. Listen to Your Christmas Cards

Every year families give and receive Christmas cards. Most of us tend to open them, glance at the name of the sender, look carefully for a personal message, and then toss each card aside. Perhaps your family displays them, rather than just keeping them in a drawer or bowl in the family or living room. They might be used as a decoration: tacked up around the border of the living room or on the wall of a den or, perhaps, on a piece of string somewhere in the home.

But we can do much more than that. We can listen to them. We can listen to what they say and what they mean. When someone cares enough to send a card, we should be eager to hear the message. A Christmas card should mean something special.

How can you "hear" what they have to say? It is easy. Some evening, perhaps before or after dinner, your family could use the message on a particular card for a prayer. Or each member of the family could choose a card from the Christmas mail and read its contents to the family. You might talk about what was written, about the people who sent the card, and of past memories you might have shared together. All this will bring the sender and the Christmas greetings into the center of your family.

Another way a family might use their Christmas cards is to play a game of "guess who sent me." This game will send the family to the pile of cards and can also encourage the children to look at the cards and appreciate the thoughtfulness of the sender. Each player is given ten Christmas cards. When he/she gets the cards, no one else should know who each card is from. It's a big secret and the object of the game is to guess who sent the card. Each player takes a turn and says something, some personal hint, some characteristic that might let the others guess who sent the card. The other players get three guesses. Whoever guesses correctly first gets the card. If no one guesses the sender, the owner keeps the card. The player who has the most cards is the winner. With younger children the parents could give the hints and help them guess correctly as a variation of the game.

24. Lost Reindeer Game

Here is a little game that might help pass a few minutes during those long days of waiting before Christmas.

Santa Claus can't find his reindeer, and it would be terrible if they could not be found before Christmas. They're all hiding here in these letters — upside-down, backwards, diagonally. Can you help Santa Claus find his nine reindeer? Here are their names:

Comet	R	D	U	C	P	S	V	C	K	J
Cupid	S	O	C	P	O	I	O	U	B	W
Donder	O	H	U	R	E	M	K	X	L	O
Blitzen	D	P	P	N	E	Z	T	I	L	B
Dasher	L	L	I	T	C	D	A	V	R	E
Dancer	L	O	D	P	R	A	N	C	E	R
Prancer	I	D	A	N	C	E	R	O	Z	T
Vixen	M	U	C	R	X	H	J	M	D	G
Rudolph	P	R	E	I	P	O	Z	T	U	D
	B	V	V	R	E	H	S	A	D	N

25. The Jesse Tree

"But a shoot shall sprout from the stump of Jesse, and from his roots a bud shall blossom" (Is 11:1). This is an ancient Old Testament quotation referring to one of the ancestors of Jesus. All of Chapter 11 of Isaiah (you might want to read it) is about the rule of Emanuel, God-with-us.

The Jesse Tree is another seasonal tradition which recalls the family tree of Christ. Just as children like to know about their parents, grandparents, and great-grandparents, they like to know about Christ's family tree. In the making of the tree, you look for symbols that can stand for important people or events, either in Christ's life or connected to him before his birth.

The "tree" can be made out of many things. You can use an actual tree limb, one from an apple tree would be especially nice. Or it can be done on a piece of felt or burlap or a large piece of construction paper. All members of the family can participate in making symbols from construction paper or light cardboard to represent the genealogy of Christ.

You may think of others, but here are some symbols and names that can be used on your Jesse Tree:
— King David (use a crown)
— Adam (the father of all men; use an apple)
— Noah (ark)

- Jacob (ladder)
- Moses (10 commandments)
- Joseph (a coat of many colors)
- Mary and Joseph
- Ruth (wheat or corn)
- Holy Spirit (a dove)
- Birthday candle
- Christ (Chi Rho)

Attach a string or colored ribbon and hang the symbol from the branch, or paste it on your burlap, felt, etc. Perhaps you might spend time having each person explain why he/she chose the symbol used. Use your own creative abilities to think of additional symbols. You can use the symbols year after year on your Jesse Tree. They also can be transferred to the Christmas tree on Christmas Eve.

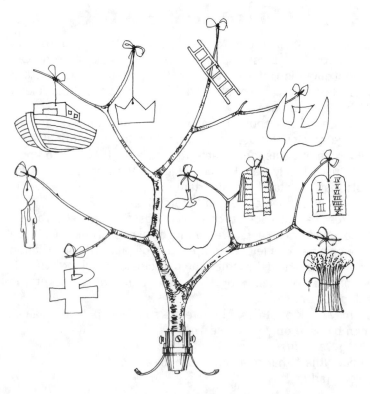

26. Special Christmas Play

During Advent we prepare gifts for our family, friends, and neighbors. We give gifts to remind us of the gift that God sent us at the time of the first Christmas. He sent his own Son to share our human life. What do our gifts say?

The following little play can be used before opening Christmas gifts, perhaps a few days before, or very close to the actual time of opening gifts.

1st Reader: (Places, near the crib, a gift he has made.) My gift says, "Thank you." Thank you for your friendship, your companionship, your love. Thank you for the talking we do, the games we've played together, the times you've helped me.

All: Thank you, heavenly Father, for our family, friends, and neighbors.

2nd Reader: (Places an apple near the crib.) My gift says "I'm sorry." I'm sorry for all the times I've been unkind, when I would not help, when I've said angry words to hurt you. Can you see I want to make it up? Have you noticed me trying?

All: We are sorry, heavenly Father, for the times we have broken your law of love. We have hurt the ones you gave us to love.

3rd Reader: (Places a flower near the crib.) My gift says, "Please." Please stay and be my friend. I want to share my life with you even more.

All: Heavenly Father, share your gift of life with us. Teach us to be open to your gifts and your love.

4th Reader: (Places a lighted candle near the crib.) My gift says, "I love you." Thank you for loving me. From you I learn what God's love is.

All: Heavenly Father, thank you for your love. Thank you for sending your Son, Jesus Christ, so we can see your love in a human person. Thank you for showing your love in all the people I love, and all the people who love me. Amen.

27. A Very Personal "Thank You"

This is the final activity in our Advent booklet. Your family could have a little "thank you" party or celebration. It could take place during the week between Christmas and New Year's, when life gets a bit dull again and we have little to look forward to.

For those at home, have someone in the family bake a cake or cookies and make hot cocoa. Try and set aside a special time to gather the family together to compose "thank yous" for those people who sent gifts.

For those away from home, you might use last year's Christmas cards to make your own "thank you" notes. Construction paper can be used, especially of different colors. Cut out sayings from the cards or pictures, paste them on the construction paper, write a brief note, and mail them, a perfect way to say "thank you."

Instead of writing a note for a relative away from home, plan a family "thank you" by phone so everyone can talk to the absent member or members. You might think of making a small collage. Use scenes from old magazines that might show how grateful you are for the gifts you received. Lots of other projects like this might come to mind. Do it and see how pleased a friend or relative will be with such a personal "thank you."

Conclusion

This booklet began by saying that Advent was a time to wait, to grow, and to hope. We trust that the prayers and activities gathered here have helped your family or class or you as an individual.

During this time of waiting, these prayers and activities can help make the weeks pass more quickly. They can contribute to your growth — as you learn more about your faith, your heritage, and your Redeemer, Jesus Christ. They can intensify your hope — by making you one with the millions of people who lived before you and who so patiently waited and hoped for the coming of Christ.

Of course, there are many other prayers and activities that might be done. So, use your creativity. Allow your thoughts to run wild to create new things. Let your children, at home or in the classroom, escape from the captivity of television to a new life of doing things for others. Your Advent activities are limited only by your imagination and the time you have available.

Your busy Advent will prepare you for that great season of Christmas, when you can rejoice in the fulfillment of the prophecy: " 'The virgin shall be with child and give birth to a son, and they shall call him Emmanuel,' a name which means 'God is with us' " (Mt 1:23).

A blessed and merry Christmas to all.